C000272055

Christian Liturgy

You are holding a reproduction of an original work that is in the public domain in the United States of America, and possibly other countries.You may freely copy and distribute this work as no entity (individual or corporate) has a copyright on the body of the work.This book may contain prior copyright references, and library stamps (as most of these works were scanned from library copies).These have been scanned and retained as part of the historical artifact.

This book may have occasional imperfections such as missing or blurred pages, poor pictures, errant marks, etc. that were either part of the original artifact, or were introduced by the scanning process. We believe this work is culturally important, and despite the imperfections, have elected to bring it back into print as part of our continuing commitment to the preservation of printed works worldwide. We appreciate your understanding of the imperfections in the preservation process, and hope you enjoy this valuable book.

CHRISTIAN LITURGY.

FOR THE

USE OF THE CHURCH.

By
Frederic Henry Hedge.

BOSTON:
CROSBY, NICHOLS, AND COMPANY,
111 WASHINGTON STREET.
1853.

HARVARD COLLEGE LIBRARY

1855 Sept 17

Gift

Rev Caleb Davis Bradlee

of North Cambridge

Entered according to Act of Congress, in the year 1853, by
CROSBY, NICHOLS, AND COMPANY,
in the Clerk's Office of the District Court of the District of Massachusetts.

CAMBRIDGE:
METCALF AND COMPANY, STEREOTYPERS AND PRINTERS.

CONTENTS.

ORDER OF SERVICES.

MORNING.

1. Introductory Exercise.
2. Salutation and Te Deum.
3. Scripture Lesson.*
4. Voluntary by the Choir.
5. Morning Prayer.
6. Hymn.
7. Sermon.
8. Singing.
9. Benediction.

EVENING.

1. Scriptural Induction.
2. Hymn.
3. Evening Prayer.
4. Voluntary on the Organ.
5. Scripture Lesson.*
6. Hymn.
7. Sermon, or Lecture, or Addresses.
8. Singing.
9. Benediction.

---

* It was deemed unnecessary to designate in this book the Scripture for the day. The great days of the Church will naturally suggest appropriate lessons. For the rest, it is recommended that a portion of the Gospels be read every morning. Other parts of the New Testament, or a portion of the Old Testament, in the afternoon.

INTRODUCTORY EXERCISES.

To be performed by the Minister and Choir in alternate parts, or read by the Minister alone, or chanted by the Choir.

FROM THE PSALMS.

I.

Venite, exultemus Domino.

O, COME, let us sing unto the Lord: let us heartily rejoice in the strength of our salvation.

Let us come before his presence with thanksgiving; and show ourselves glad in him with psalms.

For the Lord is a great God; and a great king above all gods.

In his hand are all the corners of the earth; and the strength of the hills is his also.

The sea is his, and he made it; and his hands prepared the dry land.

O, come, let us worship, and fall down, and kneel before the Lord our Maker.

1

For he is the Lord our God; and we are the people of his pasture, and the sheep of his hand.

O, worship the Lord in the beauty of holiness; let the whole earth stand in awe of him.

For he cometh, for he cometh, to judge the earth:

With righteousness shall he judge the world, and the people with his truth.

II.

Jubilate Deo.

O, BE joyful in the Lord, all ye lands; serve the Lord with gladness, and come before his presence with a song.

Know ye that the Lord, he is God; it is he that hath made us, and not we ourselves; we are his people, and the sheep of his pasture.

Enter into his gates with thanksgiving, and into his courts with praise; be thankful unto him, and bless his name.

For the Lord is gracious; his mercy is everlasting, and his truth endureth from generation to generation.

III.

Cantate Domino.

O, SING unto the Lord a new song; for he hath done marvellous things.

With his own right hand, and with his holy arm, hath he gotten himself the victory.

The Lord hath made known his salvation; his righteousness hath he openly shown in the sight of the nations.

He hath remembered his mercy and his truth toward the house of Israel; and all the ends of the world have seen the salvation of our God.

Show yourselves joyful unto the Lord, all ye lands; sing, rejoice, and give thanks.

Let the sea make a noise, and all that therein is; the round world, and they that dwell therein.

Let the floods clap their hands, and let the hills be joyful together before the Lord:

For he cometh to judge the earth; with righteousness shall he judge the world, and the people with equity.

IV.

Deus misereatur.

GOD be merciful unto us, and bless us; and show us the light of his countenance, and be merciful unto us:

That thy way may be known upon earth, thy saving health among all nations.

Let the people praise thee, O God; let all the people praise thee.

O, let the nations be glad, and sing for joy; for

thou shalt judge the people righteously, and govern the nations upon earth.

Let the people praise thee, O God; let all the people praise thee.

Then shall the earth bring forth her increase; and God, even our own God, shall bless us.

God shall bless us; and all the ends of the earth shall fear him.

V.

Levavi oculos meos.

I WILL lift up mine eyes unto the hills, from whence cometh my help.

My help cometh from the Lord, who hath made heaven and earth.

He will not suffer thy foot to be moved; he that keepeth thee will not slumber.

Behold, he that keepeth his people shall neither slumber nor sleep.

The Lord is thy keeper; the Lord is thy shade upon thy right hand.

The sun shall not smite thee by day, nor the moon by night.

The Lord shall preserve thee from all evil; he shall preserve thy soul.

The Lord shall preserve thy going out and thy coming in, from this time forth, and even for evermore.

VI.

Quam dilecta.

How lovely are thy tabernacles, O Lord of hosts!

My soul longeth, yea, even fainteth for the courts of the Lord; my heart and my flesh cry out for the living God.

As the sparrow findeth a house, and the swallow a nest, where she may lay her young, so let me dwell at thine altars, O Lord of hosts, my king and my God.

Blessed are they that dwell in thy house; they will be still praising thee.

Blessed are the men whose strength is in thee; in whose heart are thy ways,

They will go from strength to strength, till every one of them appeareth in Zion before God.

For a day in thy courts is better than a thousand. I had rather be a doorkeeper in the house of my God, than to dwell in the tents of ungodliness.

For the Lord God is a sun and a shield; the Lord will give grace and glory; no good thing will he withhold from them that walk uprightly.

O Lord of hosts, blessed is the man that trusteth in thee.

1*

VII.

Exaltabo te, Deus.

I WILL extol thee, O God, my King; and I will bless thy name for ever and ever. Every day will I bless thee, and I will praise thy name for ever and ever.

Great is the Lord, and greatly to be praised; and his greatness is unsearchable. One generation shall praise thy works to another, and shall declare thy mighty acts.

I will speak of the glorious honor of thy majesty, and of thy wondrous works; and men shall speak of the might of thy terrible acts, and declare thy greatness.

The Lord is gracious and full of compassion, slow to anger, and of great mercy. The Lord is good to all, and his tender mercies are over all his works.

All thy works shall praise thee, O Lord; and thy saints shall bless thee. They shall speak of the glory of thy kingdom, and talk of thy power; to make known to men his mighty acts, and the glorious majesty of his kingdom.

Thy kingdom is an everlasting kingdom; and thy dominion endureth through all generations.

The Lord upholdeth all that fall, and raiseth up all that be bowed down.

The eyes of all wait upon thee; and thou givest them their meat in due season. Thou openest thy hand, and satisfiest the desire of every living thing.

The Lord is righteous in all his ways, and holy in all his works.

The Lord is nigh unto all them that call upon him, to all that call upon him in truth. He will fulfil the desire of them that fear him; he also will hear their cry, and save them.

My mouth shall speak the praise of the Lord; and let all flesh bless his holy name for ever and ever.

VIII.

Domine, Refugium.

LORD, thou art our refuge in all generations. Before the mountains were brought forth, or ever thou hadst formed the earth and the world, even from everlasting to everlasting thou art God.

Thou remandest man to the dust, and sayest, Return, ye children of men!

For a thousand years are in thy sight as yesterday past, and as a watch in the night.

Thou bearest them away as with a flood; they are like a dream.

As grass springeth up in the morning, so man in

the morning flourisheth and groweth up; in the evening he is cut down and withereth.

Our years are spent as a tale that is told.

The days of our years are threescore years and ten, and though by reason of strength they be fourscore years, yet is their strength labor and sorrow; it vanisheth soon and we pass away.

So teach us to number our days that we may give our hearts unto wisdom.

O, replenish us speedily with thy mercy, that we may rejoice and be glad all our days. Give us joy for the days wherein thou hast afflicted us and the years wherein we have seen evil.

Let the favor of the Lord our God be upon us, and prosper thou the work of our hands; yea, the work of our hands, O, prosper thou it!

IX.

Domine probasti.

O LORD, thou hast searched me and known me; thou knowest my downsitting and mine uprising; thou understandest my thought afar off.

Thou compassest my path and my lying down, and art acquainted with all my ways!

Before the word is on my tongue, behold, O Lord, thou knowest it altogether. Thou hast beset me behind and before and layest thine hand upon me.

Such knowledge is too wonderful for me; it is high, I cannot attain unto it.

Whither shall I go from thy spirit, or whither shall I flee from thy presence?

If I ascend up into heaven, thou art there. If I make my bed in the under-world, behold, thou art there. If I take the wings of the morning and dwell in the uttermost parts of the sea, even there shall thy hand lead me and thy right hand shall hold me.

If I say, Surely the darkness shall cover me, even the night shall be light about me.

Yea, the darkness hideth not from thee, but the night shineth as the day. Yea, the darkness and the light are both alike to thee.

I will praise thee, for I am fearfully and wonderfully made. Marvellous are thy works, and that my soul knoweth right well.

How precious also are thy thoughts unto me, how great the sum of them! If I should count them they are more in number than the sand. When I awake I am still with thee.

Search me, O God, and know my heart; try me, and know my thoughts; and see if there be any wicked way in me, and lead me in the way everlasting.

X.

Quemadmodum desiderat.

As the hart panteth or the water-brooks, so panteth my soul for thee, O God!

My soul thirsteth for God, for the living God.
When shall I come and appear before God? For I
have gone with the multitude. I went with them
to the house of God, with the voice of joy and
praise, with a multitude that kept holy-day.

Why art thou cast down, O my soul? and why art
thou disquieted within me? Hope thou in God, for I
shall yet praise him for the help of his countenance.

Deep calleth unto deep with the voice of thy cat-
aracts! All thy waves and thy billows have gone
over me. But the Lord will command his loving-
kindness by day and his song in the night.

My prayer is unto the God of my life. I will say
to God, Thou art my defence.

Why art thou cast down, O my soul? Why art
thou disquieted within me? Hope thou in God,
for I shall yet praise him who is the health of my
countenance and my God.

XI.

Benedic anima mea.

BLESS the Lord, O my soul; and all that is within me bless his holy name.

Bless the Lord, O my soul, and forget not all his benefits.

Who forgiveth all thine iniquities; who healeth all thy diseases;

Who redeemeth thy life from destruction; who crowneth thee with loving-kindness and tender mercies.

The Lord is merciful and gracious; slow to anger, and of great mercy.

He hath not dealt with us after our sins, nor rewarded us according to our iniquities.

As the heaven is high above the earth, so great is his mercy toward them that fear him.

As far as the east is from the west, so far hath he removed our transgressions from us.

Like as a father pitieth his children, so the Lord pitieth them that fear him.

For he knoweth our frame; he remembereth that we are dust.

The Lord hath prepared his throne in the heavens; and his kingdom ruleth over all.

Bless the Lord, ye his angels that excel in strength; that do his commandments, hearkening unto the voice of his word.

Bless ye the Lord, all ye his hosts; ye ministers of his that do his pleasure.

Bless the Lord, all his works, in all places of his dominion. Bless the Lord, O my soul.

XII.

Non nobis Domine.

Not unto us, O Lord, not unto us, but unto thy name give glory, for thy mercy and for thy truth's sake.

Wherefore should the heathen say, Where is now their God? Our God is in the heavens; he hath done whatsoever he pleased.

Ye that fear the Lord, trust in the Lord; he is their help and their shield.

He will bless them that fear the Lord, both small and great. Ye are blessed of the Lord, which made heaven and earth.

The heaven, even the heavens, are the Lord's; but the earth hath he given to the children of men.

The dead praise not the Lord, neither any that go down into silence; but we will bless the Lord, from this time forth and for evermore. Praise ye the Lord.

XIII.

De profundis clamavi.

Out of the depths have I cried unto thee, O Lord.

Lord, hear my voice; let thine ears be attentive to the voice of my supplications.

If thou, Lord, shouldest mark iniquities, O Lord, who shall stand?

I wait for the Lord, my soul doth wait, and in his word do I hope.

Let Israel hope in the Lord; for with the Lord there is mercy, and with him is plenteous redemption.

And he shall redeem his people from all their iniquities.

XIV.

Cœli enarrant.

THE heavens declare the glory of God, and the firmament showeth his handiwork.

Day unto day uttereth speech, and night unto night showeth knowledge.

There is no speech nor language, and their voice is not heard:

Yet is their sound gone out through all the earth, and their words to the end of the world.

The law of the Lord is perfect, restoring the soul:

The testimony of the Lord is sure, making wise the simple:

The commandment of the Lord is pure, enlightening the eyes:

The judgments of the Lord are true and righteous altogether.

Who can understand his errors? Cleanse thou me from secret faults.

2

Keep back thy servant also from presumptuous sins; let them not have dominion over me.

Then shall I be upright, and I shall be innocent from the great transgression.

Let the words of my mouth, and the meditation of my heart, be acceptable in thy sight, O Lord, my strength and my redeemer.

X V.

Dominus regit me.

THE Lord is my shepherd; I shall not want.

He maketh me to lie down in green pastures; he leadeth me beside the still waters.

He restoreth my soul; he leadeth me in the paths of righteousness for his name's sake.

Yea, though I walk through the valley of the shadow of death, I will fear no evil; for thou art with me; thy rod and thy staff they comfort me.

Thou preparest a table before me in the presence of my enemies; thou anointest my head with oil; my cup runneth over.

Surely, goodness and mercy shall follow me all the days of my life; and I will dwell in the house of the Lord for ever.

XVI.

Domini est terra.

THE earth is the Lord's, and the fulness thereof; the world, and they that dwell therein.

For he hath founded it upon the seas, and established it upon the floods.

Who shall ascend into the hill of the Lord? and who shall stand in his holy place?

He that hath clean hands and a pure heart; that hath not lifted up his soul unto vanity, nor sworn deceitfully. He shall receive the blessing from the Lord, and righteousness from the God of his salvation.

Lift up your heads, O ye gates! and be ye lifted up, ye everlasting doors! and the King of glory shall come in.

Who is this King of glory? The Lord, strong and mighty; the Lord, mighty in battle.

Lift up your heads, O ye gates! even lift them up, ye everlasting doors! and the King of glory shall come in.

Who is this King of glory? The Lord of hosts, he is the King of glory.

XVII.

Afferte Domino.

GIVE unto the Lord, O ye mighty, give unto the

Lord glory and strength: give unto the Lord the glory due unto his name.

Worship the Lord in the beauty of holiness.

The voice of the Lord is upon the waters; the God of glory thundereth; the Lord is upon many waters; the voice of the Lord is powerful; the voice of the Lord is full of majesty; the Lord sitteth upon the flood; yea, the Lord sitteth King for ever.

The Lord will give strength unto his people; the Lord will bless his people with peace.

XVIII.

Deus noster refugium.

God is our refuge and strength; a very present help in trouble.

Therefore will not we fear, though the earth be removed, and though the mountains be carried into the midst of the sea: though the waters thereof roar and be troubled, though the mountains shake with the swelling thereof.

There is a river, the streams whereof shall make glad the city of God, the holy place of the tabernacles of the Most High. God is in the midst of her; she shall not be moved; God shall help her, and that right early.

The Lord of hosts is with us: the God of Jacob is our refuge.

XIX.

Exaltare.

BE thou exalted, O God, above the heavens; let thy glory be above all the earth.

My heart is fixed, O God, my heart is fixed; I will sing and give praise.

I will praise thee, O Lord, among the people; I will sing unto thee among the nations; for thy mercy is great unto the heavens, and thy truth unto the clouds.

Be thou exalted, O God, above the heavens; let thy glory be above all the earth.

XX.

Qui regis Israel.

GIVE ear, O Shepherd of Israel, that leadest thy people like a flock; thou that dwellest between the cherubim, shine forth; stir up thy strength, and come and save us.

Turn us again, O God, and cause thy face to shine; and we shall be saved.

Return, we beseech thee, O God of hosts! look down from heaven, and behold, and visit this vine; and the vineyard which thy right hand hath planted, and the branch that thou madest strong for thyself. Let thy hand be upon the man of thy right hand, upon the son of man whom thou madest strong for thyself. So will not we go back from thee; quicken us, and we will call upon thy name.

Turn us again, O Lord of hosts! cause thy face to shine, and we shall be saved.

XXI.

Confiteantur.

O THAT men would praise the Lord for his goodness, and for his wonderful works to the children of men!

For he hath broken the gates of brass, and cut the bars of iron in sunder.

They that go down to the sea in ships, that do business in great waters, these see the works of the Lord, and his wonders in the deep.

For he commandeth, and raiseth the stormy wind, which lifteth up the waves thereof.

They mount up to the heaven, they go down again to the depths: their soul is melted because of trouble.

Then they cry unto the Lord in their trouble, and he bringeth them out of their distresses. He maketh the storm a calm, so that the waves thereof are still.

He turneth the wilderness into a fruitful land, and dry ground into water-springs; and there he maketh the hungry to dwell, that they may prepare a city for habitation.

He blesseth them, so that they are multiplied greatly, and suffereth not their cattle to decrease.

Again, they are minished and brought low, through oppression, affliction, and sorrow. He poureth contempt on princes, and causeth them to wander in the wilderness, where there is no way.

Yet setteth he the poor on high from affliction, and maketh him families like a flock. The righteous shall see it and rejoice, and all iniquity shall stop her mouth.

Whoso is wise, and will observe these things, even they shall understand the loving-kindness of the Lord.

O that men would praise the Lord for his goodness, and for his wonderful works to the children of men. O, give thanks unto the Lord, for he is good; for his mercy endureth for ever.

XXII.

Laudate.

O, PRAISE the Lord, all ye nations; praise him, all ye people.

For his merciful kindness is great toward us; and the truth of the Lord endureth for ever.

The Lord is my strength and song, and is become my salvation; the voice of rejoicing and salvation is in the tabernacles of the righteous.

Open to me the gates of righteousness; I will go into them, and I will praise the Lord.

This is the day which the Lord hath made: we will rejoice and be glad in it. Blessed is he that cometh in the name of the Lord.

O, give thanks unto the Lord, for he is good; for his mercy endureth for ever.

XXIII.

Laetatus sum.

I WAS glad when they said unto me, Let us go into the house of the Lord.

Our feet shall stand within thy gates, O Jerusalem.

Pray for the peace of Jerusalem; they shall prosper that love thee.

Peace be within thy walls, and prosperity within thy palaces.

For my brethren and companions' sake, I will now say, Peace be within thee.

Because of the house of the Lord our God I will seek thy good.

XXIV.

Ad te levavi.

UNTO thee lift I up mine eyes, O Thou that dwellest in the heavens!

Behold, as the eyes of servants look unto the hand of their masters, and as the eyes of a maiden unto the hand of her mistress, so our eyes wait upon the Lord our God, until that he have mercy upon us.

They that trust in the Lord shall be as Mount Zion, which cannot be removed, but abideth for ever.

As the mountains are round about Jerusalem, so the Lord is round about his people, from henceforth even for ever.

XXV.

Laudate Dominum.

PRAISE ye the Lord; for it is good to sing praises unto our God; for it is pleasant, and praise is comely.

The Lord doth build up Jerusalem; he gathereth together the outcasts of Israel. He healeth the broken in heart, and bindeth up their wounds.

Great is our Lord, and of great power; his understanding is infinite.

Sing unto the Lord with thanksgiving, sing praise upon the harp unto our God.

He covereth the heaven with clouds; he prepareth rain for the earth; he maketh grass to grow upon the mountains.

He giveth to the beast his food, and to the young ravens which cry.

The Lord taketh pleasure in them that fear him, in those that hope in his mercy.

Praise the Lord, O Jerusalem! Praise thy God, O Zion! For he hath strengthened the bars of thy gates; he hath blessed thy children within thee.

XXVI.

Cantate Domino.

SING unto the Lord a new song, and his praise in the congregation of the saints. Let Israel rejoice in him that made him; let the children of Zion be joyful in their King.

Praise God in his sanctuary! Praise him in the firmament of his power! Praise him for his mighty acts! Praise him according to his excellent greatness! Praise him with the sound of the trumpet! Praise him with the psaltery and harp! Let every thing that hath breath praise the Lord! Praise ye the Lord!

MISCELLANEOUS.

XXVII.

O LORD, thou art my God: I will exalt thee, I will praise thy name. For thou hast been a strength to the poor, a strength to the needy in his distress, a refuge from the storm, a shadow from the heat; and thou wilt take away the veil that is spread over all nations; thou wilt swallow up death in victory.

Thou wilt keep him in perfect peace whose mind is stayed on thee. Trust ye in the Lord for ever; for in the Lord our God is everlasting strength.

Thus saith the Lord, the Holy One of Israel. In returning and rest shall ye be saved; in quietness and confidence shall be your strength: the work of righteousness shall be peace, and the effect of righteousness quietness and assurance for ever.

And the redeemed of the Lord shall return and come to Zion with songs and everlasting joy upon their heads: they shall obtain joy and gladness; and sorrow and sighing shall flee away.

XXVIII.

COMFORT ye, comfort ye, my people, saith your God. Speak ye comfortably to Jerusalem, and cry unto her that her warfare is accomplished, that her iniquity is pardoned; for she hath received of the Lord's hand double for all her sins.

The voice of him that crieth in the wilderness, Prepare ye the way of the Lord; make straight in the desert a highway for our God.

Every valley shall be exalted, and every mountain

and hill shall be made low; and the crooked shall be made straight, and the rough places plain.

And the glory of the Lord shall be revealed, and all flesh shall see it together: for the mouth of the Lord hath spoken it.

O thou that tellest good tidings to Zion, get thee up into the high mountain! O thou that tellest good tidings to Jerusalem, lift up thy voice with strength! lift it up; be not afraid. Say unto the cities of Judah, Behold your God!

How beautiful upon the mountains are the feet of him that bringeth good tidings, that publisheth peace; that bringeth good tidings of good, that publisheth salvation; that saith unto Zion, Thy God reigneth!

Break forth into joy! Sing together, ye waste places of Jerusalem! For the Lord hath comforted his people; he hath redeemed Jerusalem; and all the ends of the earth shall see the salvation of our God!

XXIX.

Ho, every one that thirsteth, come ye to the waters! and let him that hath no money come, buy and eat: yea, come, buy wine and milk, without money and without price.

Incline your ear, and come unto me: hear, and your soul shall live.

Seek ye the Lord while he may be found: call ye upon him while he is near.

Let the wicked forsake his way, and the unrighteous man his thoughts; and let him return unto the Lord, and he will have mercy upon him; and to our God, for he will abundantly pardon.

Ye shall go out with joy, and be led forth with peace: the mountains and the hills shall break before you into singing, and all the trees of the field shall clap their hands.

Instead of the thorn shall come up the fir-tree; and instead of the brier shall come up the myrtle-tree; and it shall be to the Lord for a name, for an everlasting sign, that shall not be cut off.

The Lord shall comfort Zion; he shall comfort her waste places; and make her like Eden, like the garden of the Lord.

Joy and gladness shall be found therein; thanksgiving, and the voice of melody.

XXX.

BLESSED are the poor in spirit; for theirs is the kingdom of heaven.

Blessed are they that mourn; for they shall be comforted.

Blessed are the meek; for they shall inherit the earth.

3

Blessed are they that hunger and thirst after righteousness; for they shall be filled.

Blessed are the merciful; for they shall obtain mercy.

Blessed are the pure in heart; for they shall see God.

Blessed are the peacemakers; for they shall be called the children of God.

Blessed are they that are persecuted for righteousness' sake; for theirs is the kingdom of heaven.

Blessed are ye, when men shall revile you, and persecute you, and shall say all manner of evil against you falsely, for my sake.

Rejoice, and be exceeding glad; for great is your reward in heaven; for so persecuted they the prophets that were before you.

Come unto me, all ye that labor and are heavy laden, and I will give you rest.

Take my yoke upon you, and learn of me; for I am meek and lowly in heart; and ye shall find rest unto your souls.

For my yoke is easy, and my burden is light.

XXXI.

I HEARD a voice from heaven, saying unto me, Write, "Blessed are the dead who die in the Lord, from henceforth."

Yea, saith the Spirit, that they may rest from their labors; and their works do follow them.

And I saw a new heaven and a new earth; for the first heaven and the first earth were passed away. And I heard a great voice out of heaven, saying, Behold, the tabernacle of God is with men, and he will dwell with them, and they shall be his people; and God himself shall be with them, and be their God.

And God shall wipe away all tears from their eyes; and there shall be no more death, neither sorrow, nor crying, neither shall there be any more pain; for the former things are passed away.

And he that sat upon the throne said, It is done. I am the beginning and the end. I will give unto him that is athirst, of the fountain of the water of life freely. He that overcometh shall inherit all things; and I will be his God, and he shall be my son.

And the Spirit and the Bride say, Come. And let him that heareth say, Come. And let him that is athirst come. And whosoever will, let him take the water of life freely.

XXXII.

FOR THANKSGIVING.

(From Psalm lxv. *Te decet.*)

PRAISE is due to thee, O God, in Zion, and to thee shall the vow be performed.

Blessed is he whom thou choosest, and causest to approach unto thee, that he may dwell in thy courts. O, satisfy us with the blessings of thy house, even of thy holy temple.

By wonderful deeds dost thou answer us in thy goodness, O God of our salvation, who art the confidence of all the ends of the earth, and of them that are afar off upon the seas.

Thou makest fast the mountains by thy strength, being girded with power. Thou stillest the noise of the seas, the roar of their waves, and the tumult of the people.

They also that dwell in the uttermost parts of the earth are amazed at thy tokens. Thou makest the realms of the morning and evening to rejoice.

Thou visitest the earth and waterest it. Thou enrichest it exceedingly. The river of God is full of water. Thou suppliest the earth with corn when thou hast thus prepared it.

Thou waterest the furrows thereof abundantly; Thou settlest the ridges thereof; Thou makest it soft with showers, and blessest the springing thereof.

Thou crownest the year with thy goodness, thy footsteps drop plenty. They drop it upon the pastures of the wilderness, and the hills all around rejoice; the pastures are clothed with flocks, and the valleys are covered with corn; they shout and they sing for joy.

XXXIII.

FOR CHRISTMAS.

Magnificat.

MY soul doth magnify the Lord, and my spirit hath rejoiced in God my Saviour.

For he hath regarded the low estate of his handmaiden.

For, behold, from henceforth all generations shall call me blessed.

For he who is mighty hath magnified me, and holy is his name.

And his mercy is on them that fear him, throughout all generations.

He hath shown strength with his arm, he hath scattered the proud in the imagination of their hearts.

He hath put down the mighty from their seats, and hath exalted the humble and the meek.

He hath filled the hungry with good things, and the rich hath he sent empty away.

He, remembering his mercy, hath holpen his servant Israel, as he promised to our forefathers, to Abraham and his seed for ever.

XXXIV.

FOR CHRISTMAS.

Gloria in excelsis.

GLORY be to God in the highest, on the earth peace, good-will toward men.

Blessed are the people that know the joyful sound; they shall walk, O Lord, in the light of thy countenance;

Through the tender mercies of our God, whereby the dayspring from on high hath visited us;

To give light to those that sit in darkness and in the shadow of death, and to guide our feet in the way of peace.

How beautiful upon the mountains are the feet of him that bringeth good things; that publisheth peace, that bringeth good tidings of good; that publisheth salvation; that saith unto Zion, Thy God reigneth.

There is sprung up a light for the righteous, and joyful gladness for such as are true of heart.

Rejoice in the Lord, ye righteous, and give thanks at the remembrance of his holiness.

Sing unto the Lord and praise his name; be telling of his salvation from day to day.

Let all those that seek him be joyful and glad in him, and let all such as love his salvation say always, The Lord be praised.

XXXV.

For Easter.

Christ our passover is sacrificed for us; therefore let us keep the feast:

Not with the old leaven, neither with the leaven of malice and wickedness, but with the unleavened bread of sincerity and truth.

Christ being raised from the dead dieth no more: death hath no more dominion over him.

For in that he died, he died unto sin once, but in that he liveth, he liveth unto God.

Likewise reckon ye yourselves to be dead indeed unto sin, but alive unto God through Jesus Christ our Lord.

Christ is risen from the dead and become the first fruits of them that slept. For since by man came death, by man came also the resurrection of the dead. For as in Adam all die, even so in Christ shall all be made alive.

Blessing and honor and glory and power be unto him who sitteth upon the throne, and unto the Lamb for ever and ever. Amen.

SALUTATION.

(*The Congregation rise.*)

Min. The Lord be with you all.
Con. And with thy Spirit.
Min. Lift up your hearts.
Con. We lift them up unto the Lord.
Min. Let us give thanks unto the Lord.
Con. It is right and just.

TE DEUM LAUDAMUS.

(*To be repeated by the Congregation after the Minister.*)

WE praise thee, O God, we acknowledge thee to be the Lord.

All the earth doth worship thee, the Father everlasting.

To thee all angels cry aloud, the heavens and all the powers therein.

To thee cherubim and seraphim continually do cry.

Holy, holy, holy Lord God of hosts! Heaven and earth are full of the majesty of thy glory.

The glorious company of the Apostles praise thee.

The goodly fellowship of the Prophets praise thee.

The noble army of martyrs praise thee.

The holy Church throughout the world doth acknowledge thee;

The Father of an infinite majesty;

Thine adorable true and only Son;

Also the Holy Ghost the Comforter.

Thou art the King of Glory, O Christ!

Thou art the everlasting Son of the Father.

When thou hadst overcome the sharpness of death, thou didst open the kingdom of Heaven to all believers.

Thou sittest at the right hand of God, in the glory of the Father.

We pray thee, help thy servants whom thou hast redeemed with thy most precious blood.

Make them to be numbered with thy saints in glory everlasting.

O Lord God, save thy people and bless thy heritage.

Govern them and lift them up for ever.

Day by day we magnify thee;

And we worship thy name ever, world without end.

Vouchsafe, O Lord, to keep us this day without sin.

O Lord, have mercy upon us, have mercy upon us.

O Lord, let thy mercy be upon us as our trust is in thee.

O Lord, in thee have we trusted; let us never be confounded.

(The Congregation sit.)

MORNING PRAYER.

EXHORTATION.

BELOVED in the Lord, our hearts admonish us
that we are not sufficient to ourselves, nor able of
ourselves to satisfy the manifold wants and requirements of our imperfect natures. Our sufficiency
is of God, who alone is able to give us the things
which we need, to deliver us from evil, and to make
us truly blest. Therefore, seeing we are instructed
by our holy religion to come freely to the throne
of Grace, and to make our requests unto God by
prayer and supplication, with thanksgiving; and
are assured that the Lord is nigh unto them that
call upon him, unto all who call upon him in truth; I
invite you, as many as are here present, to unite with
me in common prayer to our Heavenly Father, that
he of his fulness and infinite good-will would graciously bestow upon us those needed mercies and
comfortable gifts which we are emboldened to ask
in Christ, who is the Way; giving thanks unto God
through him.

(Congregation rise or kneel.)

O Lord, have mercy upon us, have mercy upon us.

O Lord, let thy mercy be upon us as our trust is in thee.

O Lord, in thee have we trusted; let us never be confounded.

(The Congregation sit.)

MORNING PRAYER.

EXHORTATION.

BELOVED in the Lord, our hearts admonish us that we are not sufficient to ourselves, nor able of ourselves to satisfy the manifold wants and requirements of our imperfect natures. Our sufficiency is of God, who alone is able to give us the things which we need, to deliver us from evil, and to make us truly blest. Therefore, seeing we are invited by our holy religion to come near to the Throne of Grace, and to make our sincere wish and prayer and supplication with thankful heart, and are assured that the Lord is nigh unto all who call upon him, unto all who call upon him I invite you, as many as are here present, to unite with me in common prayer to our Heavenly Father, that he of his fulness and infinite goodness would graciously bestow upon us those sacred blessings and comfortable gifts which we so much desire, and which in Christ, who is the Way, he alone can send us through him.

(*Congregation rises and sits.*)

Then may follow the Litany below, or the Stated Collects, or an original Prayer, at the discretion of the Minister.

LITANY.

Min. O God, our Heavenly Father, have mercy upon us.

Con. O God, our Heavenly Father, have mercy upon us.

Min. O God, by thy Christ, the Redeemer of the world, have mercy upon us.

Con. O God, by thy Christ, the Redeemer of the world, have mercy upon us.

Min. O God, by thy Holy Spirit, the Comforter, Teacher, and Guide of mankind, have mercy upon us.

Con. O God, by thy Holy Spirit, the Comforter, Teacher, and Guide of mankind, have mercy upon us.

Min. Forgive, O Lord, our manifold, sins and offences. We have erred and strayed from thy ways; we have left undone those things which we ought to have done, and have done those things which we ought not to have done. We pray thee to remove our transgressions from us; spare thou those who confess their faults; restore thou those that are penitent, according to thy promises declared unto mankind in Christ Jesus our Lord.

Con. Spare us, good Lord.

Min. From all evil and mischief; from sin, from the crafts and assaults of the adversary; from thy wrath and from everlasting death;

Con. Good Lord, deliver us.

Min. From all blindness of heart; from pride, vainglory, and hypocrisy, from envy, hatred, and malice, and all uncharitableness;

Con. Good Lord, deliver us.

Min. From all inordinate and sinful affections, and from all the deceits of the world, the flesh, and the devil;

Con. Good Lord, deliver us.

Min. From the fury of the elements, from plague, pestilence, and famine; from battle and murder and death unprepared for;

Con. Good Lord, deliver us.

Min. From all sedition and civil discord, from all false doctrine and unbelief, from hardness of heart and contempt of thy word and commandment;

Con. Good Lord, deliver us.

Min. In all time of our tribulation; in all time of our prosperity; in the hour of death, and in the day of judgment;

Con. Good Lord, deliver us.

Min. We beseech thee, O Lord, that it may please thee to rule and guide and comfort thy holy Church universal, to bring into the way of truth all

4

such as have erred and are deceived, to send worthy
laborers into thy vineyard, and to give saving power
to the preaching of thy word.

Con. We beseech thee to hear us, good Lord.

Min. That it may please thee to illumine all
ministers of the Gospel and teachers of truth, and
to give to them, and to the people committed to
their charge, the needful spirit of thy grace, and to
pour out upon them the continual dew of thy
blessing.

Con. We beseech thee to hear us, good Lord.

Min. That it may please thee to bless and preserve all rulers and magistrates, and all who are in
authority over us, giving them grace to execute jus-
tice and to maintain truth.

Con. We beseech thee to hear us, good Lord.

Min. That it may please thee to bless all sorts
and conditions of men, to make known thy ways
unto all people, thy saving health to all nations; to
give to all nations unity, peace, and concord, a
heart to love and fear thee, and diligently to live
after thy commandments.

Con. We beseech thee to hear us, good Lord.

Min. That it may please thee to give to all thy
people increase of grace to hear thy word, to receive
it with pure affection, and to bring forth the fruits
of the spirit, that all who profess and call themselves Christians may hold the faith in unity of

spirit, in the bond of peace, and in righteousness of life.

Con. We beseech thee to hear us, good Lord.

Min. That it may please thee to strengthen such as do stand, to comfort and help the weak-hearted, and to raise up those who fall.

Con. We beseech thee to hear us, good Lord.

Min. That it may please thee to succor, help, and comfort all who are in danger, necessity, or tribulation.

Con. We beseech thee to hear us, good Lord.

Min. That it may please thee to minister unto such as are any ways afflicted or distressed in mind, body, or estate, to comfort and relieve them according to their need, giving them patience under their trials, and a happy issue out of all their afflictions.

Con. We beseech thee to hear us, good Lord.

Min. That it may please thee to preserve all who travel by land or by water, all women in the perils of childbirth, all sick persons and young children, and to show thy pity upon all prisoners and captives.

Con. We beseech thee to hear us, good Lord.

Min. That it may please thee to defend and provide for the fatherless and widows, and all who are desolate and oppressed.

Con. We beseech thee to hear us, good Lord.

Min. That it may please thee to have
upon all men.

Con. We beseech thee to hear us, good L

Min. That it may please thee to forgiv
enemies, persecutors, and slanderers, and tc
their hearts.

Con. We beseech thee to hear us, good L

Min. That it may please thee to give an
serve to our use the kindly fruits of the ea
that in due time we may enjoy them.

Con. We beseech thee to hear us, good L

Min. That it may please thee to sanctify
thy Holy Spirit, to make us perfect in every
work, and to keep us blameless unto the end.

Con. We beseech thee to hear us, good L

Min. The Lord bless us and keep us.

Con. The Lord cause his face to shine up

Min. The Lord lift up the light of his cc
nance upon us.

Con. And give us peace.

Occasional petitions, such as the Collect for the day, on the great
the Church, or any special petition which the Minister may wish to
shall be read or said here. After that, or immediately after the fore

THE LORD'S PRAYER.

(To be repeated by the Congregation after the Minister.)

Our Father who art in heaven, hallowed t
name. Thy kingdom come, thy will be do

earth as it is in heaven. Give us this day our daily bread. Forgive us our trespasses, as we forgive them that trespass against us. And lead us not into temptation, but deliver us from evil. For thine is the kingdom and the power and the glory, for ever and ever. Amen.

Min. Glory be to the Father, and to the Son, and to the Holy Ghost;

Con. As it was in the beginning, is now, and ever shall be, world without end.

4*

EVENING PRAYER.

Min.   The Lord be with you.

Con.   And with thy spirit.

Min.   Lift up your hearts.

Con.   We lift them up unto the Lord.

Min.   Wherewith shall I come before the Lord, and bow myself before the most high God?

Con.   He hath showed thee, O man, what is good; and what doth the Lord require of thee, but to do justly, and love mercy, and walk humbly before God?

Min.   Let us search and try our ways, and let us turn again unto our God.

Con.   Search me, O God, and know my heart, try me and know my thoughts; and see if there be any wicked way in me.

Min.   If we say we have no sin, we deceive ourselves, and the truth is not in us.

Con.   If we confess our sins, God is faithful and just to forgive our sins and to cleanse us from all unrighteousness.

Min. Let us therefore come boldly to the throne of Grace, that we may obtain mercy and find grace to help in time of need.

Con. I will take the cup of salvation, and call upon the name of the Lord.

Min. Let the wicked forsake his way and the unrighteous man his thoughts, and let him return unto the Lord, and he will have mercy upon him, and to our God, and he will abundantly pardon him.

Con. Turn thou us unto thee, O Lord! and we shall be turned.

Min. Who can understand his errors? Cleanse thou me from secret faults.

Con. Create in me a clean heart, O God, and renew a right spirit within me.

Min. Blessed is he whom thou choosest and causest to approach unto thee.

Con. Blessed are the pure in heart, for they shall see God.

Min. Return unto thy rest, O my soul, for the Lord hath dealt graciously with thee.

Con. I will arise and go to my Father.

Min. Let us pray. O Lord, have mercy upon us!

Con. And grant us thy salvation.

Then shall be said the following prayer, or, if the Minister prefer it, an original prayer, or the Stated Collects.

Min. O God, most holy, just, and true, we
seech thee, absolve us from all our sins, and fre
from all uncleanness of the flesh and the sp
Grant that we truly repent of all the evil
have at any time committed; that we put a
from us all unrighteous thoughts, and all un
desires and affections, and faithfully endeavo
correct our faults and reform our lives. May
put off the old man of the former conversation,
rupt with deceitful lusts, and be renewed in
spirit of our mind, and put on the new man, w
is fashioned according to God in righteousness
true holiness. O Lord, have pity on our wave
wills, and mercifully consider our infirmity. F(
will is present with us, but how to perform
which is good, we find not: the good that we wc
we do not; but the evil which we would not,
we do. Deliver thou us from the grievous rul
passion in our hearts, and redeem us from the
in our members which warreth against the lav
our minds. From evil concupiscence, from in(
nate affection, from undue love of self and the w(
from covetousness, from envy, hatred, and all
charitableness, from unlawful desires, impure im
nations, and carnal excess, from the waste of
time, from evil words and corrupt communicati
good Lord, deliver us. Redeem us from the bon(
of corruption into the glorious liberty of the (

dren of God, that we not only delight in thy law with the inward man, but obey it in our lives, and being made free from sin may become servants unto God, living soberly, righteously, and godly in this present world, having peace for the fruit of obedience, and the end everlasting life. Amen.

If there be any special petition or collect or original aspiration to be offered, it shall be presented here. In the absence of such, or immediately thereafter, shall be said the following sentences.

Min. O Lord, open thou our eyes!

Con. That we may know the mysteries of the kingdom of heaven.

Min. O Lord, open thou our ears!

Con. That we may hear thy word with heed, and receive it with pure affection.

Min. O Lord, open thou our lips!

Con. And our mouth shall show forth thy praise.

Min. Now unto the King eternal, immortal, invisible, the only wise God;

Con. Be honor and glory through Jesus Christ, for ever and ever.

Min. Praise ye the Lord.

Con. The Lord's name be praised.

SCRIPTURAL INDUCTIONS.

THE Lord reigneth, let the earth rejoice. Righteousness and judgment are the pillars of his throne. Enter into his gates with thanksgiving and into his courts with praise, be thankful unto him and bless his name.

The eyes of all wait upon thee, and thou givest them their meat in due season. Thou openest thine hand and satisfiest the desire of every living thing. The Lord is righteous in all his ways and holy in all his works. The Lord is nigh unto all them that call upon him, unto all that call upon him in truth. My mouth shall speak the praise of the Lord, and let all flesh bless his name for ever and ever.

I will come into thine house in the multitude of thy mercies, and in thy fear will I worship at thy holy temple. Give ear to my words, O God, consider my meditation. Hearken unto the voice of my cry, my King and my God; for unto thee will I pray. Let the words of my mouth and the meditation of my heart be acceptable in thy sight, O Lord, my strength and my redeemer.

Praise is due to thee, O God, in Zion, and unto thee shall the vow be performed. O Thou that hearest prayer, unto thee shall all flesh come. Blessed is the man whom thou choosest and causest to approach unto thee : we shall be satisfied with the goodness of thy house, even of thy holy temple. My soul waiteth upon God; from him cometh my salvation.

And the voice said, Cry. What shall I cry? All flesh is grass, and all the goodliness thereof as the flower of the field. The grass withereth, the flower fadeth, but the word of the Lord endureth for ever. And this is the word which by the Gospel is preached unto you.

Ye are not come unto the earthly mount, that burned with fire, nor unto blackness and darkness and tempest. But ye are come unto Mount Zion and unto the city of the living God, the heavenly Jerusalem, and to an innumerable company of angels, to the general assembly and church of the first-born which are written in heaven, and to God the Judge of all, and to the spirits of just men made perfect, and to Jesus the Mediator of the new covenant. Wherefore gird up the loins of your mind, be sober, and hope to the end for the grace that is offered you in the revelation of Jesus Christ.

I say unto you, that in this place is one greater than the temple. Know ye not that ye are the temple of God, and that the spirit of God dwelleth in you?

Stand in the gate of the Lord's house, and proclaim there this word, and say, Hear ye the word of the Lord, all ye that enter in at these gates to worship the Lord. Thus saith the Lord of hosts: Amend your ways and your doings, and I will cause you to dwell in this place. For I spake not unto your fathers concerning burnt-offerings and sacrifices; but this thing I commanded them, saying, Obey my voice, and I will be your God, and ye shall be my people.

There remaineth therefore a rest for the people of God. Let us labor to enter into that rest. Come unto me, all ye that labor and are heavy laden, and I will give you rest. Take my yoke upon you and learn of me, for I am meek and lowly, and you shall find rest unto your souls.

THE STATED COLLECTS.

At the close of each Collect, the Congregation shall say, Amen.

THE COLLECT FOR GRACE.

O GOD, from whom all holy desires, all good counsels, and all just works do proceed, defend us now and ever by thy mighty power; and grant that we fall into no sin, neither run into any kind of danger; but that all our doings may be ordered by thy governance to do always that which is righteous in thy sight, through Jesus Christ our Lord. *Amen.*

THE COLLECT FOR MERCY.

WE humbly beseech thee, O Father, mercifully to look upon our infirmities; turn from us all those evils to which we are liable, and grant that in all our troubles we may put our whole confidence and trust in thy mercy, and evermore serve thee in holiness and pureness of living, to thy honor and glory. *Amen.*

The Collect for Aid.

O Lord, our Heavenly Father, almighty and everlasting God, assist us in all our doings with thy most gracious favor, and further us with thy continual help, that in all our works begun, continued, and ended in thee, we may glorify thy holy name, and by thy mercy obtain everlasting life, through Jesus Christ our Lord. *Amen.*

The Collect for Peace.

O God, who art the author of peace and the lover of concord; in knowledge of whom standeth our eternal life, whose service is perfect freedom; give unto us that peace which the world cannot give, that our hearts may be set to obey thy commandments. And graciously defend us in all the assaults of our enemies, that we, surely trusting in thy defence, may not fear the power of any adversaries, and that, hurt by no persecutions, we may pass our time in rest and quietness, and evermore give thanks unto thee in thy holy Church, through Jesus Christ our Lord. *Amen.*

A Prayer for all Conditions of Men.

O God, the creator and preserver of all mankind, we humbly beseech thee, for all sorts and conditions of men, that thou wouldst be pleased to make thy ways known unto them, thy saving health unto all nations. More especially we pray for thy holy Church Universal; that it may be so guided and governed by thy good Spirit, that all who profess and call themselves Christians may be led into the way of truth, and hold the faith in unity of spirit and the bond of peace, and in righteousness of life. Finally, we commend to thy fatherly goodness all those who are any ways afflicted or distressed in mind, body, or estate; that it may please thee to comfort and relieve them according to their several necessities; giving them patience under their sufferings, and a happy issue out of all their afflictions. *Amen.*

If there be any special prayer or collect to be offered, it shall be presented here.

A General Thanksgiving.

ALMIGHTY God, Father of all mercies, we, thine unworthy servants, do give thee most humble and hearty thanks for all thy goodness and loving-kindness to us and to all men; we bless thee for our creation, preservation, and all the blessings of this life, but above all for thine inestimable love in the redemption of the world by our Lord Jesus Christ; for the means of grace and for the hope of glory. And we beseech thee, give us that due sense of all thy mercies, that our hearts may be unfeignedly thankful, and that we may show forth thy praise, not only with our lips, but in our lives, by giving up ourselves to thy service, and by walking before thee in holiness and righteousness, all our days, through Jesus Christ our Lord, in whose name we ascribe unto thee all honor and glory. *Amen.*

A Concluding Prayer.

ALMIGHTY God, who hast given us grace at this time with one accord to make our common supplications unto thee, and hast promised by thy beloved Son, that, where two or three are gathered together in thy name, thou wilt grant their requests; fulfil now, O Lord, the desires and petitions of thy servants as may be most expedient for them, granting us in this world knowledge of thy truth, and in the world to come life everlasting. *Amen.*

THE grace of our Lord Jesus Christ, and the love of God, and the fellowship of the Holy Ghost, be with us all evermore. *Amen.*

SPECIAL COLLECTS.

For Advent.

Almighty God, give us grace that we may cast away the works of darkness, and put on the armor of light now in the time of this mortal life, in which thy Son Jesus Christ did visit us in great humility; that when he shall come again in his glory we may reign and rise through him to life immortal. And this we beg in the name of the Mediator, through whom we ascribe unto thee all honor and glory now and ever. *Amen.*

For Christmas.

Almighty God, who hast given us thy only begotten Son to take our nature upon him, and as at this time to be born of woman, grant that we, being regenerate and made thy children by adoption and grace, may be daily renewed by thy Holy Spirit. And this we beg in the name of Jesus Christ, through whom we ascribe unto thee all honor and glory, now and ever. *Amen.*

For the First Sunday in the Year.

O God, the unfailing source of life and mercy, who hast brought us to the beginning of this year, and art sparing us to love thee and to keep thy commandments; give us, we beseech thee, a solemn sense of the importance of time, and of diligence in improving the talents thou hast placed in our hands; and enable us so faithfully to discharge our duty in this life, that we may finally attain to that eternal kingdom which thou hast promised by Jesus Christ our Lord. *Amen.*

For Lent.

We beseech thee, O Father, who delightest in mercy, and art not willing that any should perish, to grant unto us the pardon of all our sins, and a joyful hope of thine approbation; and to assist us in forsaking all our evil ways, and returning to the path of thy commandments, that we may obtain everlasting life, through Jesus Christ our Lord. *Amen.*

For Good Friday.

Almighty and everlasting God, who of thy tender love for mankind hast sent thy Son, our Saviour Jesus Christ, to take upon him our flesh, and to suffer death upon the cross, that all mankind should follow the example of his great humility, mercifully grant that we may follow the example of his patience, and so be made partakers of his resurrection, through the same Jesus Christ our Lord. *Amen.*

For Easter.

O MERCIFUL God, who by thy Son Jesus Christ hast overcome death and opened unto us the gates of everlasting life, grant that we, thy servants, having this hope, may purify ourselves even as he is pure; and by continually mortifying our corrupt affections, may pass the grave and gate of death to our joyful resurrection; which we ask as disciples of Him who died and was buried and rose again for us, thy Son, Jesus Christ our Lord. *Amen.*

For Whitsunday.

GOD, who as at this time didst teach the hearts of thy faithful people by the sending to them the light of thy Holy Spirit, grant us by the same Spirit to have a right judgment in all things, and evermore to rejoice in the holy comfort of the same Spirit, through Jesus Christ our Saviour, in whose name we ascribe unto thee all honor and glory now and for ever. *Amen.*

For All-souls-day.

O GOD, the protector of all who trust in thee,

without whom nothing is strong, nothing is holy, in whom our fathers trusted and in whom they rest, increase and multiply upon us thy mercy, that, thou being our ruler and guide, we may so pass through things temporal, that we finally lose not the things eternal. Grant this, O Heavenly Father, through Jesus Christ our Lord. *Amen.*

Before or after Sermon.

Blessed Lord, who hast caused all holy Scriptures to be written for our instruction, grant that we may in such wise hear them, read, mark, learn, and inwardly digest, that by patience and comfort of thy holy word we may embrace and ever hold fast the blessed hope of everlasting life which thou hast given us in our Saviour Jesus Christ. *Amen.*

Another.

O almighty God, who alone canst order the wills and affections of men, grant unto thy people that they may love the thing which thou commandest, and desire that which thou dost promise, that so among the sundry and manifold changes of this world our hearts may surely there be fixed, where alone true joys are to be found, through Jesus Christ our Lord. *Amen.*

ANOTHER.

LORD of all power and might, who art the Author and Giver of all good things, graft in our hearts the love of thy name, increase in us true religion, nourish us with all goodness, and of thy great mercy keep us in the same, through Jesus Christ our Lord. *Amen.*

ANOTHER.

ALMIGHTY God, the Fountain of all wisdom, who knowest our necessities before we ask, and our ignorance in asking, we beseech thee to have compassion on our infirmities, and grant that those things which we faithfully ask may be effectually obtained, and those things which for our unworthiness we dare not, and for our blindness we cannot ask, vouchsafe to give us for the sake of thine infinite mercy in Jesus Christ our Lord. *Amen.*

COMMUNION SERVICE.

[NOTE. — This service may begin and proceed with singing, address, reading, or prayer, at the discretion of the minister. The Liturgy embraces only the concluding or cenatory act. In a service so liable to excess of formality, it was judged best to leave a wide margin for such voluntary exercises or such spontaneous expressions of thought and devotion as the Minister or Church may be moved to connect with it.]

EUCHARISTIC LITURGY.*

Min. The grace of our Lord Jesus Christ, the love of God the Father, and the communion of the Holy Ghost, be with you all.

Comm. And with thy spirit.

Min. Lift up your hearts.

Comm. We lift them up unto the Lord.

Min. Let us praise the Lord.

Comm. It is meet and just.

Min. Yea, it is meet and just and seemly and profitable, day and night, with lips never silent, and

---

* After the old Greek Liturgies, with especial use of that of Antioch, called the Liturgy of St. James.

heart never dumb, to praise and to bless and to give thanks unto thee, O Lord, who madest heaven and earth, the sea and all that in them is; who madest man in thine own image, and when he had transgressed didst not overlook him nor forsake him, but didst recall him by thy Law and school him by thy Prophets, and didst fashion and renew· him by the awful and heavenly mysteries of religion; who madest all things by thy Wisdom, the true Light, thine only begotten Son, our Saviour Jesus Christ, through whom we render unto thee the reasonable service which is rendered, O Lord, by all thy people from north to south, from the rising of the sun to the going down of the same; through whom every rational creature worshippeth and sendeth up unto thee the eternal song of praise.

Angels, Archangels, Thrones, Dominions, Principalities, Authorities, and Powers; Cherubim and Seraphim call one to another with ceaseless voice, and repeat the triumphal hymn, singing and shouting, and saying:

Comm. Holy, holy, holy Lord God of hosts, heaven and earth are full of thy glory.

Min. Wherefore, together with the heavenly host, we also cry aloud and say, Holy indeed art thou, all-holy, and without measure is the majesty of thy holiness. Holy also is thine only begotten Son, our Lord Jesus Christ, and holy the Spirit that searcheth all things, yea, the deep things of God.

Thou didst send thy Son into the world that he might renew and reanimate thine image. Who, born of woman, and having his conversation with men, did order all things pertaining to the salvation of our race. And being about to undergo the voluntary and life-giving death upon the cross, — the sinless for us sinners, — on the night in which he was betrayed, — let us rather say, in which he delivered up himself for the life and salvation of the world:

Taking bread in his holy and innocent and immortal hands, he blessed it and brake, and gave to his disciples, saying: Take, eat, this is my body, which is broken and given for you for the remission of sins.

Comm. Amen.

Min. Also taking the cup after he had supped, and blessing it and giving thanks, filled with the Holy Ghost, he gave it to his disciples, saying: Drink ye all of it; this is the blood of the New Covenant, which is shed for you and for many, and given for the remission of sins.

Comm. Amen.

Min. This do in remembrance of me. For as oft as ye eat of this bread and drink of this cup, ye show forth the death of the Son of Man, and declare his resurrection, until he come.

Comm. Thy death, O Lord, we show forth, and declare thy resurrection.

Min. We, therefore, mindful of his life-giving doctrines, his saving cross and death, his burial and resurrection, his ascension and seat at the right hand of God, — we set apart and devote to the memory of Christ this bread and this cup. And we beseech thee, O Lord, to sanctify these elements, and to sanctify us with thy holy presence. And may this bread be unto us as the sacred body of thy Christ.

Comm. Amen.

Min. And may this cup be unto us as the honored blood of thy Christ.

Comm. Amen.

Min. That so this rite may be profitable to all who partake of it, for the remission of sins, for eternal life, for the sanctification of body and soul, for fruitfulness in good works, for the stablishing of thy holy Church which thou hast founded on the rock of faith, that the gates of hell may not prevail against it. May we who thus eat of one bread and drink of one cup be made one with each other in the fellowship of the same Holy Spirit, and one with thee in Christ.

And in this our communion we remember, and beseech thee to remember and to bless, the multitudes of every name who are joined with us in one household of faith, — our brethren and sisters in Christ throughout the world.

6

We remember those who have fallen asleep in Christ, and in the joyful hope of resurrection unto life eternal. O Lord, refresh their spirits with the light of thy countenance.

We remember the fathers from the beginning of the world; the patriarchs, prophets, apostles, martyrs, and all who have wrought righteousness, from righteous Abel even to the present day. Refresh thou their spirits, and give them abundant entrance into the joy of our Lord. And grant unto us, O God, that we may have our part and lot with all thy saints.

We remember all such as journey or are about to journey, and them that sojourn in strange lands. May they have thee for their fellow-voyager and fellow-traveller. May it please thee to abide with them wheresoever they abide, and whether they travel by land or by water, to bring them in safety to their destined goal. Abide with those whom they leave behind, and grant that, in health remaining, they may welcome their own in health returning, and rejoice with them in safety and in peace.

We remember all who are sick and in distress, all who suffer in body or in mind, all who are in prison and in bonds. As bound with them, and as sufferers with them, we bear them in our hearts and pray for their relief.

We remember our enemies, if there be any who

have injured us, or any who look upon us with evil eye, and cherish hatred against us. We beseech thee to turn their hearts, and that we may live peaceably with all men. May we freely forgive all who have wronged us; and if there be any whom we have wronged, may we make amends and seek forgiveness.

We remember the whole family of man, beseeching thee that the spirits of all flesh may taste of thy grace, and that the ends of the earth may see the salvation of God.

And unto us, O Lord, vouchsafe such guidance, that as Christians, and blameless, we may spend the remainder of our life. Gather us, O Lord, when thou wilt, and as thou wilt, but be it without shame and without reproach, through Jesus Christ our Lord, who alone was found sinless on earth.

Comm. Put away from us, O Lord, our sins, whether wilful or against our wills, in deed and in word, in knowledge and in ignorance, in mind and disposition, forgive them all according to thy mercy;

Min. In Jesus Christ thy Son, in whom and through whom we bless thee now and ever.

Comm. Amen.

Min. O God and Father of our Lord Jesus Christ, may it please thee to accept us in these our supplications. May our offerings find favor in thy sight, and be as the odor of spiritual incense. Accept them, O Lord, as thou didst accept the offerings of holy men of old, and bless them as thou didst bless the centurion's alms and the widow's mite. Sanctify us with the grace of thy Christ, and with the frequency of thy Holy Spirit. Sanctify soul and body and spirit, and make us worthy to call upon thee, the Father in heaven, and to say:

Comm. Our Father who art in heaven, hallowed be thy name. Thy kingdom come, thy will be done on earth as in heaven. Give us this day our daily bread. Lead us not into temptation, but deliver us from evil.

Min. Yea, Lord, lead us not into temptation, but deliver us from evil. For thy mercy knoweth that we, through much weakness, are not able of ourselves to overcome. But do thou, together with the trial, provide also a way of escape. For thou givest thy servants power to tread upon serpents and scorpions, and on all the power of the enemy. For thine is the kingdom, and the power, and the glory, for ever and ever.

Comm. Amen.

Min. Peace be with you.

Comm. And with thy spirit.

Then the Minister, taking in his hands the bread and the cup, shall say:—

To the Father of lights, from whom cometh down every good and every perfect gift, rendering unto

God the things which are God's, we consecrate these gifts of his love, these memorials of our Lord, the holy to the Holy.

Comm. One is holy, and one is our Master, even Christ, to the glory of God the Father.

Then the Minister shall break the bread, and shall say : —

Beloved in the Lord, I deliver unto you that which I have received of the Lord Jesus, the bread and the cup of Christian Communion.

Then, delivering the bread, having first himself partaken thereof, he shall say : —

Take and eat this in remembrance of Christ.

Then, delivering the cup, having first himself partaken thereof, he shall say : —

Drink this in remembrance of Christ.

And after the Communicants have received the elements, the Minister shall say this prayer : —

O God, who with great and unspeakable love hast condescended to our weakness, and hast vouchsafed unto us to partake of this heavenly board, enter not into judgment with us, thy servants, but guard us in the sanctity of thy Holy Spirit, that being holy we may find part and inheritance with all the holy who in all time have well pleased thee, in the light of thy countenance; through the grace of thine only begotten Son, our Lord Jesus Christ.

Comm. Amen.

If there be any special petition to be offered, or event to be commemorated, it shall be done here.

CONCLUDING PRAYER.

Min. O Thou great and adorable God, look down upon thy servants who now bow before thee; stretch forth thine hand full of power and of blessing, and bless thy people. Guard thine inheritance, that ever and everywhere we may glorify thee, the only living and true God, and thy Son and thy Holy Spirit, world without end.

Comm. Amen.

Then may follow a hymn, or remarks, at the discretion of the Minister; and after that, or without them, the

BENEDICTION.

THE RITE OF BAPTISM.

WHEN our Lord Jesus Christ sent forth his disciples, charged with the ministry of his Gospel, he gave them commandment, saying: "Go ye, therefore, and teach all nations, baptizing them in the name of the Father, and of the Son, and of the Holy Ghost."

The ordinance of Baptism, thus divinely instituted, has been perpetuated through all the ages of the Christian dispensation, and continues to this day to denote and to constitute the entrance into the Church of those to whom it is administered. It is the act whereby believers, by right of faith, and the children of believers, by right of inheritance, are formally enrolled and incorporated as members of the body of Christ.

The use of water in this sacrament is symbolic. As water is the universal purifier, so it is intended by the use of this element to typify that spiritual purification, that cleansing of the inward man from sin and pollution, which the Church, through the ministry of the Holy Spirit, imparts to believers and to the children of believers.

If it be an infant that is to be baptized, the minister shall further say to the parents or sponsors :—

Christian parents who offer their children to be baptized, present them to the Lord, and devote them to his service, acknowledging in these little ones a divine original, a spiritual nature, a heavenly calling, and an immortal destiny ; and engaging, or expressing their intent, to secure to them the benefits of Christian instruction, and to bring them up in the nurture and admonition of the Lord.

Then shall the Minister say : —

Which things being duly considered, let the water of Baptism now be administered.

And he shall baptize the child or the adult, pronouncing the baptismal name, and saying :—

I baptize thee in the name of the Father, the Son, and the Holy Ghost.

After this a prayer shall be offered, and then, if convenient, a hymn may be sung.

THE RITE OF CONFIRMATION.

The individual to be confirmed, that is, admitted into the communion of the Church, shall have first received the Sacrament of Baptism, if not as infant, or at some subsequent period, then now, as candidate for confirmation. To such baptized persons as may wish to join the communion of the Church, the Minister shall say, in the presence of the Church : —

Is it your desire and intent to enter the communion of the Church of Christ? Do you believe in the religion of Jesus Christ as taught in the Scriptures of the New Testament? Do you receive it as Divine, and accept it as the rule of life and the way of salvation?

Then shall he cause such person or persons to kneel, saying unto them : —

Kneel and receive the blessing of the Church.

Then he shall lay his hands upon the head of each one so kneeling, and say : —

Defend, O Lord, this thy servant with thy heavenly grace ; that he (*she*) may continue thine for ever, and daily increase in thy Holy Spirit more and more ; and may an abundant entrance be administered unto him (*her*) into thine everlasting kingdom. *Amen.*

Then shall he say : —

The Lord be with you.

Ans.   And with thy spirit.

Min.   Let us pray.

Almighty and everlasting God, who workest in us to will and to do, we make our supplications unto thee for these thy servants, whom thou hast called by thy grace to be partakers of the life and privileges of the Christian Church. Give unto them, O Lord, remission of sins. Strengthen them, we beseech thee, with the Holy Ghost, and daily increase in them thy manifold gifts of grace, the spirit of wisdom and understanding, the spirit of counsel and strength, of knowledge and true godliness. Let thy fatherly hand, we beseech thee, be always over them; let thy Holy Spirit be always with them; and so lead them in the knowledge and obedience of thy word, that they may obtain everlasting life. Almighty God, vouchsafe, we beseech thee, to direct, sanctify, and govern both our hearts and our bodies in the ways of thy laws, and in the works of thy commandments, that through thy gracious protection, here and ever, we may be preserved in body and soul, through our Lord and Saviour Jesus Christ. *Amen.*

BENEDICTION.

The blessing of God, the grace of our Lord Jesus Christ, and the fellowship of the Spirit, be with you ever. *Amen.*

MARRIAGE SERVICE.

ADDRESS.

FRIENDS, we have assembled here to sole
the nuptials of this man and this woman, wl
sign to become one in holy wedlock, pledging
mutual faith, in a solemn covenant before God
they will henceforth live together, after God's
nance, as husband and wife.

For wedlock is the ordinance of God, wh
that it was not good for man to be alone, and
fore created him male and female, and inst
marriage as the ground of human fellowshi
beginning of society, and the mother of mai
For this cause, it is written, shall a man
father and mother, and shall cleave unto his
and they two shall be one flesh.

And this estate our holy religion has mac
symbol of a higher than earthly alliance, typ
by it the soul's espousal with the Heavenly
groom.

Seeing, therefore, that marriage is of God, let us hallow it in our thoughts, and attend these rîtês, as a sacrament of religion, with seriously disposed and reverent minds.

Then, addressing the parties to be united in marriage, the Minister shall say: —

M. and N., — Ye stand here mutually betrothed, and ye purpose to enter the holy estate of matrimony. Know that the covenant which ye now make with each other and with God, and to which ye pledge your mutual faith, engages you, as far as in you lies, to be helpers of each other's joy and comforters of each other's sorrow, to cleave one to another with holy affection and unwavering constancy so long as you both shall live. See to it, therefore, that ye are fully persuaded in your own minds, and that ye know of no impediment by reason of which ye may not be lawfully married.

Then shall the Minister say to the man: —

M., wilt thou have this woman to thy wedded wife, to live together, after God's ordinance, in the estate of matrimony? Wilt thou love her, comfort her, honor and keep her, in sickness and in health, in good days and in evil days, and, knowing no other as wife, cleave only unto her so long as ye both shall live?

7

Then shall the Minister say to the woman : —

N., wilt thou have this man to thy wedded husband, to live together, after God's ordinance, in the estate of matrimony? Wilt thou love him, comfort him, honor and keep him, in sickness and in health, in good days and in evil days, and, knowing no other as husband, cleave only unto him so long as ye both shall live?

Then shall he cause them to join their right hands, saying : —

If such be the purpose of your hearts, then join your right hands in token thereof.

Then shall be said a prayer, which may be the following, or such other, instead thereof, as the Minister may be moved to offer : —

O Eternal God, Creator and Preserver of all mankind, Giver of all good, Fountain of all joy! command thy blessing, we beseech thee, on these thy servants, whom we bless in thy name. Enable them to fulfil and obey the covenant which they have now made in thy presence. May their hearts be united in the closest bonds of love, may they be counsel and strength and light and comfort one to another, sharers of each other's joys, consolers of each other's sorrows, and helpers to each other in all the changes and chances of the world. May they so discharge the duties which belong to this relation into which they have entered, that it may not be to them a state of temptation and sorrow, but of holiness and comfort. Give them grace, whereby they may serve thee acceptably so long as they live. Hand in hand, and heart with heart, trusting in each other and in thee, may they tread together the path of life. Be thou, dear God, their guard and guide; give them grace to know and to serve thee aright, and lead them through this transitory life unto life eternal, according to thy rich mercy, in Jesus Christ our Lord. Amen.

Then shall the Minister say : —

Forasmuch as M. and N. have consented together in wedlock, and have witnessed the same before God and this company, and thereto have engaged and pledged themselves with the joining of hands, I pronounce them to be husband and wife. And what God has joined together, let not man put asunder.

Then shall he add this blessing : —

The Lord God Almighty bless and preserve and keep you, the Lord look mercifully upon you with his favor, and fill you with his grace, that ye may so live together in this life, that in the world to come ye may have life everlasting. Amen.

BURIAL SERVICE.

The service may begin with one or more of the following sentences: —

I AM the resurrection and the life, saith the Lord Christ. He that believeth in me, though he were dead, yet shall he live, and whosoever liveth and believeth in me shall never die.

Then shall the dust return unto the earth as it was, but the spirit shall return unto God who gave it.

Man that is born of woman is of few days, and full of trouble. He cometh forth as a flower, and is cut down; he fleeth also as a shadow, and continueth not.

I heard a voice from heaven saying unto me, Write, From henceforth blessed are the dead who die in the Lord; even so, saith the Spirit, for they rest from their labors.

For we know that if our earthly house of this tabernacle were dissolved, we have a building of God, a house not made with hands, eternal in the heavens.

Let not your heart be troubled, saith the Lord Jesus. Ye believe in God, believe also in me. In my father's house are many mansions: if it were not so, I would have told you. I go to prépare a place for you. And if I go and prepare a place for you, I will come again and receive you unto myself, that where I am, there ye may be also.

Then may follow a hymn; after that, selections from the thirty-ninth and ninetieth Psalms, and also from the fifteenth chapter of the First Epistle to the Corinthians. Then shall be offered a prayer, which may be followed by a hymn, if convenient. And the service at the church or house may close with a Benediction.

COLLECT AT A FUNERAL.

O Merciful God, the Father of our Lord Jesus Christ, who is the resurrection and the life, in whom whoso believeth shall live though he die, and whoso liveth and believeth in him shall not die eternally; who also hath taught us by his Apostle not to sorrow, as those who have no hope, for such as sleep in him; we humbly beseech thee, who didst raise up the Lord Jesus from the dead, that thou wouldst raise up us also by him from the death of sin to the life of the spirit, that when we go hence, to be here no more, we may go in peace, rejoicing in hope, yea, though we walk through the valley of the shadow of death, may fear no evil, trusting in him who giveth us the victory, through our Lord Jesus Christ. Amen.

At the grave the Minister may say : —

Forasmuch as it hath pleased Almighty God to take unto himself the soul of our departed brother (*sister*), we therefore commit his (*her*) body to the ground, earth to earth, ashes to ashes, dust to dust, in sure and certain hope that there shall be a resurrection to eternal life of all those who die in the fear and love of God; for this corruptible must put on incorruption, and this mortal must put on immortality.

He who testifieth of these things saith, Surely I come quickly ; Amen. Even so come, Lord Jesus.

The grace of our Lord Jesus Christ be with you all. Amen.

THE END.